Prometeo

Prometeo

C. Dale Young

Four Way Books
Tribeca

in memoriam Mavis Clarke (1936-2016)
and Cecil Young (1934-2015)

&

for my family

Library of Congress Cataloging-in-Publication Data

Names: Young, C. Dale, author.
Title: Prometeo : poems / C. Dale Young.
Description: Tribeca, New York : Four Way Books, [2021] | Identifiers: LCCN 2020037833 |
ISBN 9781945588709 (trade paperback)
Subjects: LCGFT: Poetry.
Classification: LCC PS3625.O96 P76 2021 | DDC 811/.6--dc23
LC record available at https://lccn.loc.gov/2020037833

This book is manufactured in the United States of America and printed on
acid-free paper.

Four Way Books is a not-for-profit literary press. We are grateful for the assistance
we receive from individual donors, public arts agencies, and private foundations.

This publication is made possible with public funds from the
National Endowment for the Arts

and from the New York State Council on the Arts, a state agency,

We are a proud member of the Community of Literary Magazines and Presses.

Contents

Do you see that tree? It is dead but it still sways in the wind with the others.

—Anton Chekhov, *The Three Sisters*

For Its Blue Flickering

If you take cobalt as a simple salt
and dissolve it—if you dip a small metal loop
in such a solution and place it in a standard

flame, it burns a brilliant blue,
the flame itself bluer than the richest of skies
in summer. I wanted to be that blue.

And so, I claimed that element as my own,
imagined that fire could make of me
something bluer than the bluest of blues.

But what does an eighteen-year-old boy know
of the blues? All I knew then of cobalt
was its stable isotope. I had no knowledge

of the radioactive one with its gamma rays
used for decades to treat cancer. I had yet
to be exposed to such a thing. I was hot

for cobalt, for its blue flickering. Chemistry
can be such an odd thing. When a teacher of mine
offered up that faggots doused in certain chemicals

burned blue, I saw it as a sign; how can we
not see such things as signs, as omens?
Blue the waters of the Caribbean Sea,

blue the skies over the high deserts,
and "blue" the passages I found in old Greek texts
that surprised my prudish sense

of what men could do with men. It always
came back to blue. But boyish ideas are just that.
They seem for all the world to be fixed things,

when all they are is fleeting. In the end,
my make up was none other than anthracite,
something cold, dark, and difficult to ignite.

It is dense, only semi-lustrous, and hardly
noticeable. One dreams in cobalt, but one lives
in anthracite. Yes, the analogy is that basic.

Anthracite, one of earth's studies in difficulty:
once lit it burns and burns. Caught somewhere
between ordinary coal and extraordinary graphite,

anthracite surprises when it burns. It isn't flashy—
it produces a short, blue, and smokeless flame
that reminds one of the heart more than the sky.

Portrait in Midnight Blue and a Widening Gyre

I wanted nothing. I was in want of nothing.
Isn't that how it always begins? Isn't that how
the mind allows the body to have what it wants?

The trees leaning in over the railing of the deck,
their leaves whispering like the friends leaning in
trying to eavesdrop—one autumn night, one smile,

one terrible fumble of hands and one bottle of wine.
The trees were interested and not remotely interested.
One kiss. One kiss on the cheek and one left to bruise

my neck like something from a bad romance novel.
But here, more than a decade later, I am still falling for you.
Can I say that now? Can I say that with a straight face?

A visit to the dunes to argue about music at midnight
—the Pacific trying its best to drown us out—was all
I needed for confirmation. I am easy that way.

But by the time you quoted Yeats to finish my
own sentence, nothing could have saved me. Sometimes,
what one least wants is what one gets. I wanted

to be alone, to have time to fall in love with myself
all over again. I wanted nothing to do with another man.
I wanted nothing. But here we are two decades later.

Out over the Pacific, the fog holds its position.
The lone ship skirts the horizon but always aware
of its final destination. And where on God's earth

are we heading? I admit it now. I admit it. See?
The final destination was never really important.
Halfway, they say, just halfway there.

And still, I want you to take me all the way.

At Lake Merced

Some men go down to the river.
I went down, instead, to the lake: the air
silent and stretched tightly over it,

the water unmoved and dangerously still.
Some men move past such a scene
without even the slightest notice of it.

But this morning, a man in a shell
rowed across this lake's smooth surface,
the tip of his shell leaving a widening V

behind it, the shell cleanly slicing through
the water like an arrow, the way an arrow slices
through air or flesh. And just like that, the image

of the Saint pierced through by arrows becomes
fixed within my head, the arrows all leaving V's
behind them, V for violence, as if the very air

were an impasto on canvas. And just like that,
the arrows slicing through the air become bullets,
each one leaving its V behind it, the paint

at the target dabbed with a red duller than crimson.
You may wonder why on earth a man shot through
centuries ago would appear to me upon seeing this

tiny shell of a boat crossing a lake, but the present day
does a remarkable job of emulating the past. Let us
leave it at that. Some men find nothing, and others

find omens everywhere. The stillness of the air
above the lake; the shell slicing through the water;
the Saint shot through with arrows yet living, breathing,

his chest heaving, his head slumping while the arms remain
perfectly still; and the brown boy shot through
with bullets, his wounds a red duller than crimson:

things like this still happen almost every day.

Transept

Unlike me, she made a choice, chose
Indian over Chinese, because she felt
she looked more Indian than Chinese.

It "takes strength" to choose. When I was five
and playing near my grandmother's feet, she
knitted sweaters for me because she was

always convinced I was cold. You smile
too much. You are too pretty for a boy, too pretty.
You will bring yourself trouble. I smiled

and laughed the way only small children do
when teased. Pretty boy with an English heart,
cold cold heart that needs warming.

I giggled at the sound of the words
"English heart." Why was she
always worrying about me? She

already knew what it meant to be
a mongrel. Cold heart. Mean heart. Icy fist
planted against the coldest marble,

marble from a place white with snow,
an island unlike anything near the Indian Ocean.
What an anomaly: an English heart

in a brown body. When she visits me now
in dreams, she is still knitting me a sweater
and teasing me about my smile, my all-too-easy

charm, my cold cold heart. But Daadee is wrong,
you see. My heart crackles. It hisses and flickers
in the dark cathedral of my chest.

Mestizaje

At the ruins of Tulum, on a boulder
half-buried in sand on the famous beach
below the often-photographed pyramid
that stares out at the sea, I found

a petroglyph overlaid in white chalk
to better demonstrate the bird-like thing
carved into the rock's side. I had seen it before.
In Cuba, maybe, or Puerto Rico, somewhere

on one of the islands out across this sea
watched over here by trees and pyramids.
The bird, on this boulder, like the one
I had seen elsewhere, had only one leg.

But this should come as no surprise, the Taino
having left this soil many hundreds of years ago
to search for new land, new coastlines.
They made landfall all across the Antilles

and flourished until the Spaniards arrived.
As the textbooks will tell you, the Taino are
extinct, the people and their culture
extinguished by Spain long ago. But tell that

to the old brujas, the old island women
who will proclaim we are of this dirt
and can send any man who stands against us
back to the dirt. The irony of this is legion.

One did not need a laboratory to cross
the tangerine with the grapefruit to make
the tangelo, and the Spaniards did not need
a laboratory to cross the Taino with themselves.

So, when I stand here on this beach at Tulum,
is it any wonder we all look like cousins?
Not the Spaniards who dabbled in the witchcraft
of mestizaje, not the Spaniards who claimed

all of this region as their own—no, it is
the Taino, cousins to the Maya, that link us.
Peer into the DNA of many Caribbean people,
and you will find that 10-20% of it

is indigenous, is Taino. We are of this dirt. We cannot
be killed off, the old women say. And in the base pairs
of our DNA, we discover the truth. One can hide
many things, but the truth is always there.

An ancient god buried himself in the dirt that gave
rise to the Taino. And with time, the Taino themselves
were buried. This is all true. But they are not dead.
No, no, not dead. They are buried within us.

The Point

His other doctors proclaimed that he would die
      within a month. He kept on living for years:
the simple fact is that he was barely thirty

      but had been dying for almost two of them.
The urge for prophecy is deep and deeply
      rooted inside the gnarled and human heart—

we seek it out, its shiny metallic edge.
      The cancer spread to his bones and then his liver.
Each time it reappeared, we treated it

      with radiation; we stalled it, held it back,
until it spread to his lungs making every treatment
      that I proposed seem less and less an option.

So this is it? You're just going to let me die?
      Mano, you leave me here to die like this?
But here, you see, the tongue is wiser than

      a knife, the word selected not just "brother" but
a word that cut far deeper than English ever could.
      The urge to prophecy is deep but not a given.

I gave no answer. I gave him nothing more.
      And when I tried to rest my hand against
his arm, he turned away from me and said

to leave him, leave him now, to which he added
mano, again, to drive the sharpened point home.
        The fact is he was barely thirty years old,

and I had failed him, run out of things to try.
        Not even I could blame him for that finely-
honed stab, that carefully-chosen Spanish word.

        To some, the owl is a symbol of death to come.
For others, it is the guardian that ferries souls.
        I'm still not sure to which one I subscribe.

But there was not an owl in sight that morning,
        barely a week since trying to talk to him,
and nothing to see outside except the dark.

        I knew that something was off, was terribly wrong,
no matter how I tried to calm my mind.
        I stood there thinking, thinking about it all:

our final conversation, my failures, what now?
        I tried to reassure myself that I
had done all that I could have done for him.

        Some of us study the future, and others the past.
It makes no difference at all. At work that day,
        his sister called to let me know he died.

He passed that morning just before the sun
        had started rising. Why I knew this then,
knew it before the news had yet to come,

        troubles me even to this day. Not English,
not "brother," bother buried within the word.
        Instead, the Spanish word he knew would leave

a mark, would slice to the bone, sharp as a knife.

Portrait in Salt and Dusky Carmine

As in childhood, the gentility of verandas
and gardens, of tea and its trappings, made me
anxious. But it took very little time for someone
to disappear from that world. The cane fields

that separate civility from the rough shoreline
allow anyone, upper crust or field hand, to disappear.
Down one of many dirt rows, the line cut as straight
as the cane planted on either side, one rushes

from the cultured world to an untouched one.
Out of the cane fields, out from their wind-rippled leaves
shepherding you onward, one finds the sand
and sea awaiting as if discarded by a retired god.

The setting sun's red and orange fingers tried,
unsuccessfully, to reconfigure the seven shades
the water's varying depths reflected, but all
that changed was the sea foam once white now pink.

The English painter, who visited here once, wrote
that the daily gaudiness of this sight made one
long for the nuance of dimming light at dusk
as it smudged its charcoal over a Hampshire field.

All I can say is it takes a certain temperament
to prefer a sunset in Hampshire to a sunset
in the Caribbean. I do not have such a temperament.
I prefer a scene that requires oils instead of charcoal.

The shore empty, the sun no longer visible,
the water's colors finally succumbed and darkened
to night, the same as that settling over us from above.
Not the sunset, but the time following sunset:

the day's Technicolor displays erased. Alone
on the soft sand, the surf mumbled the old language.
Like my great-great-grandmother who visits me
in dreams, it said: *Salt or no salt, trust no one.*

It is difficult for one like me to disregard the sea
and the cane fields. I am perfectly aware this place
is no longer my home, but the sea says *Truth is truth,*
and the cane field says *Like the machete, you belong to me.*

AMMOPHILA

in memoriam Derek Walcott (1930-2017)

That sail which leans on light,
tired of islands . . .

Who could be tired of islands, the ones among
the archipelago we call the Lesser
Antilles? Only a sail could be so tired.

I tried in vain to utilize a cluster
of sea grapes in this poem, but they belong
to you now; I am not as brazen as

I used to be. . . . Along a white sand beach
this morning, I revised the sea grapes, transformed
them into grass, the dull and common plant

that few can rightly name as *ammophila*:
as you so aptly cautioned years ago,
the naming matters as much as anything.

You see, I paid attention then despite
my face betraying boredom. Shakespeare, Homer,
I read it all and found that you were right

insisting so. And now, I cannot help
but see Odysseus on every sea,
in every billowing sail I sight off shore.

The classics? They are dead now, stripped of all
except their bones, the basic narratives.
Console yourself with this. A foolish boy

keeps writing poems because of what you taught
him: "Landscapes are never only settings;
they *are* the story, the only worthwhile story."

The ancient war continues. It never dies.

Pastiche

Deep in the fields, the greenish stalks were twice
my height, a forest for one who had not seen
the likes of oaks or birches. Sugar's vice
hung in the air, its sweetness somewhere between

a pastry and decay. In memory, the cane
opened its arms allowing a boy to escape.
But memory lies so well, the fields of cane
as much a trap as any means of escape.

Too young to wield a machete, far too young,
I vanished down the endless rows of cane,
my mother screaming out for me to stop.

The yard hands hacked out space to plant the young.
For them, what safety there among the cane.
For me, it's where I learned to beg a man to stop.

The Call

in memoriam Cecil Young

I am addicted to words, constantly ferret them away
in anticipation. You cannot accuse me of not being prepared.
I am ready for anything. I can create an image faster than

just about anyone. And so, the crows blurring the tree line;
the sky's light dimming and shifting; the Pacific cold and
impatient as ever: this is just the way I feel. Nothing more.

I could gussy up those crows, transform them
into something more formal, more Latinate, could use
the exact genus *Corvus*, but I won't. Not today.

Like any addict, I, too, have limits. And I have written
too many elegies already. The Living have become
jealous of the amount I have written for the Dead.

So, leave the crows perched along the tree line
watching over us. Leave them be. The setting sun?
Leave it be. For God's sake, what could be easier

in a poem about death than a setting sun? Leave it be.
Words cannot always help you, the old poet taught
me, cannot always be there for you no matter how you

store them away with sharpened forethought.
Not the courier in his leather sandals, his legs dark and dirty
from the long race across the desert. Not the carrier

pigeon arriving with the news of another dead Caesar
and the request you present yourself. Nothing like that.
The telephone rings. Early one morning, the telephone rings

and the voice is your mother's voice. No fanfare. Your
father's brother is dead. He died that morning. And your tongue
went silent. Like any other minor poet, you could not find

the best words, the appropriate words. Leave it be now.
You let your mother talk and talk to fill the silence. Leave it be.
All of your practiced precision, all of the words saved up

for a poem, can do nothing to remedy that now.

In Plain Sight

Alongside the twisting road to Erice, the cane fields
moved like water, the leaves and stalks bending
and rippling like water under the hand of the wind.

We had never seen sugarcane growing this way
except in the Caribbean; it had to be a mirage, a trick
of the imagination. But it was no trick, the cane

brought to Sicily by the Arabs in the Tenth Century.
Because Europe was sour, because it was addicted
to honey colonized by bacteria and its resulting toxins,

because in the many tributaries and streams of Sicily
the Arabs saw something akin to the world of sugarcane
they already understood, they planted the cane carefully.

But as each turn in the road revealed a new vista, not once
did we sight a mill, evidence sugar was in production.
Apparently, the Arabs brought sugar to Sicily,

but the Normans followed with fire and steel, the cane
growing rampant there now more a weed than a source
of golden sugar, the sweetness of predictable wealth.

By the end of the Fifteenth Century, sugar was worthless
in Sicily. Zucchero, said the Sicilians, the word a nod
to the Arabic sukkar. The Normans softened it, made it

more palatable before taking it back to France as sukere,
the word then stolen by the English to become "sugar."
God only knows how many centuries would have passed

without sugar in Europe, had it not been for the Arabs.
That evening, as we ate a pastry filled with ricotta,
the server, in the slowest of Italian, proudly explained

the filling had been made in that area for centuries,
the earliest recipe dating back to the late Tenth Century.
He pointed out there was nothing more Sicilian

than this ricotta, nothing more Sicilian at all.
We smiled at this with the knowledge gleaned earlier
that day. Sheep's milk is blended with powdered sugar

to make ricotta, sugar that arrived in Sicily mere years
before ricotta was established: still unseen, the Arabs, the men
and women who made so much of the European experiment

possible. A mere 5% of my DNA comes from the Arabian
peninsula, but sitting there eating that sweet dessert
I lifted wine to my lips and quietly toasted: Sukkar!

Portrait in Azure and Twine Unravelling

Sometimes what attracts us is nothing more
than a marker of what is wrong with us.
Ravel was heralded as a genius, a master
of Impressionism, for his use of highly repetitive
structures, his rhythmic and repetitive structures.
Who can deny the beauty of *Bolero*? Not me.

As a child, I asked my mother to listen to me
while I practiced words like *cobalt*, each one more
and more odd for their sounds, their structures,
something I was still figuring out. "Grant us
Peace," we repeated at Mass. Everything was repetitive.
And that is how it started, my trying to master

the language, the very words, fearful they would master
me, instead. *Azure, sinecure*, the long *u* had me
so early, and then the hard *t* one finds in *repetitive*,
substantive, titillation. I always needed more and more
words. Debussy once described Ravel as a man just like us,
one who understands that repetition structures

the way we move through the world, structures
our very breath, breath being that thing necessary to master
song, language, the natural world around us.
The first time I took a lover, she took time to watch me
sitting on the edge of the bed mouthing the word *more*.
After four hours, she dressed and called me repetitive,

told me the fun of it had ended, had become repetitive.
Memory, even when about something painful, structures
our worlds, structures our hearts and minds and more.
Within years of writing *Bolero*, Ravel could no longer master
music. He even lost the ability to use language. Imagine me
hearing this story. We were still new to each other, not yet *us*

but still me and you. When Ravel left this world, left us,
you told me, many thought him mad and madly repetitive
pouring the same cup of water over and over. "Listen to me,"
you said. "Music is more than the simple structures
one need master." I chose language instead of music to master,
all 171,000 words in the English language and more.

This morning, you caught me mouthing something other than *more*.
Ravel was not a man like us. Really. I just needed a new word to master.
My love, I'm repetitive. I sit here saying: "Structures, structures, structures."

Portrait in Purpura, Ice Plant, and Ecchymosis

You left your mark on me, the bruise
purplish and dark. In time, it faded.
I want to say it was variegated or
mottled or resembling the press

of a brush barely dipped in Tyrian.
Pointless, really, to give a bruise
so much weight. Leave it alone.
Let it be just a bruise on my neck.

Bruises fade. This morning, as I
walked the trail by the beach, the ice plant
had started its change, the fibrous leaves
dense green turning pale and then purple.

You understand, right? Things like this
prompt the gears in my head to start
their labor. Again. Memory needs
no such decoration, such labored desire.

What I am trying to say, what I want to say
is that I think of you at the oddest times.
The ice plant, the bruise you gave me
so long ago? Unnecessary. Work.

I have spent a long time with pen
and paper, and even now I am tentative.
Who doesn't love melodrama, sentimentality?
Love is fierce. Love is brutal and fierce.

Let me remember that. Let me forego ice plants
and bruises, sand turned weapon by the wind.
I have hidden behind the beauty of metaphors
for too long. I have been hiding for far too long.

False Start

after Jasper Johns

There is red, there is
red, there is red and some
yellow . . . Between, among,
between. What does it matter?

I have written the word
yellow, the word orange,
but they are just words
among, between, among. . . .

When I took off my shirt,
I was only playing. I was only
trying something on for size—
red red red and more red.

The brush moves, it knows
the canvas the way I have
learned to know your chest
among between: what does

it matter? What the hell
does it matter? I told you
to hold still. I wanted you
to take it, take this blue

paint, the red red red
and some yellow. This
is all I wanted, for you to hold
still, to accept the brush.

The paint is furious: the paint
is violent in my hands.
Flick of the brush. Flick of red,
some red and, yes, some yellow.

Portrait in Sugar and Simple Prayer

The language of sugar isn't difficult
to master. One learns it as easily as

any other tongue. You may not believe me,
but it is true. As a boy, lost in the cane fields,

I made a mistake (Who doesn't make mistakes?)
and, for this small error, I was punished, the sweet

sugarcane becoming weapon, becoming punisher.
Each time the man brought the body

of the cane stalk down across my back,
I cried out. Would you believe me if I told you

that today I wouldn't even whimper at such a thing?
Because now I know how to brandish a stalk,

how to bring it down as testament, how to make
the nothing of air sing before the strike. And because,

well, now I know how to accept punishment as well.
You punish or are punished. It really is that simple.

Dominus, Holy Father, I have hidden myself
in the cane field. I may have sinned. My back is bare

and in need of your administrations. Not salt
in the wound, Lord, but sugar. Sugar as sharp

as the metallic taste of blood in the mouth.
Make me regret this, Lord. Make me...

Strike me, Lord, strike me harder than any man.
Make of me something sweeter than sugar.

Partially Right

To arrange and rearrange the seven olives
on the tabletop took hours, one can imagine,
for the man we have come to know as Galileo.
Seven, because Neptune had to be a star,
and Pluto was nothing more than a speck
in the imagination. On the tabletop,
the concentric circles of ink on paper were
punctuated by these seven olives. At the center,
a small orange to represent our Sun.
Because he was right in all things heliocentric,
Galileo was also wrong. The earth may not have been
the center of the Universe but, as it turns out,
neither was our Sun. Looking at the night sky
above Vermont, we did not need telescopes
to discern the Milky Way. It was simply there
for all to see: stars, stars, and more stars littering
the blue-black ink of the sky as if the Vedic myth
about a god spilling milk or, depending
on the translation, his semen, to create the heavens
were in fact truth. But truth is never easy, is it?
Ashes to ashes, dust to dust, we know
we are of this Earth. And standing in a field,
the chill of late August coming down, what did
any of us know about truth? We are poets and writers
who have devoted ourselves to fictions, to myth, to lies.
So when a young man in a fey black jacket said
that we were made of the very dust of the stars,
I laughed. The hardened scientist in me laughed.
Because even if there were some tiny grain
of truth in it, wouldn't this young Galileo be only

partially right? There is, after all, poetry in
almost everything: the moth plunging into the sun
of a candle's flame; the way dust seems to dance
within beams of light; the way the hunger in each
of us betrays the soul. All of it, so goddamned poetic.
Seven olives on a table in a small town in Italy, Galileo
watchful and intent on them, forcing himself to divine
the workings of the heavens: even that is poetic.
Seven planets and seven gods or goddesses
to steer them through the night sky. And what of this
poor student of physics, this even poorer student
of biochemistry? This student discovers years later
that in each and every one of us, there are seven grams
of silica, seven grams of dust that came from the stars.
It is never easy, the truth. It has never been easy.
Alone now and far from Vermont, there is no one
to utter platitudes or poetry to me in the dark.
And up above me, the sky is speckled with stars.
Do they call to us the way the ocean calls
to the saltwater within us? I don't know. It isn't my job
to know. My job is to look, to look up. It is a job
our kind has had for all of our short-lived history.

Portrait in Seafoam and Offshore Lights

You do this to break people's hearts, don't you?

I didn't start this to break anyone's heart.
Last night, miles off shore, the boats could not
be seen, only their lights like small stars

low in the sky, punctuating the unseen horizon.
I want to be exact. I want to be as precise
as possible, the lights from the boats

not stars but like stars. Crab season has arrived,
and this is now a nightly occurrence.
Does this explain it to you? Does this help

you understand why I do this? Not to break
people's hearts—no, never that. Early this morning,
the sunlight creeping down the hillside, enough

light in the sky to erase the lights of the boats,
I walked down to the Pacific. Why do any of us
do the things we do? I have raised no children,

but I need to understand that kind of insanity.
Mother, I write to understand so many things,
even that rampant act of commitment. At the beach,

a small boy, maybe five, would run a hundred yards,
perhaps, and then rush back to his mother. Over and over,
the boy swinging out from her and returning.

I actually know people who write to break hearts,
but I am not one of those people. You know full well
I have had my heart broken more than once,

so it isn't out of lack of understanding the material.
To be exact, to be precise, is a kind of purity at times,
even if impossible. The stringency, the odd joy

in deploying the right word: do you see? I never did
this to break someone's heart. Time after time, I have
sought the courage, the resolve, to break my own.

Portrait in Celadon and Hymenoptera

Any insect that is neither bee nor ant
in the suborder Apocrita of the order Hymenoptera
is called a wasp. *Ptera*, for the wings they possessed,

and *Hymen*, for the fact the wings were membranous.
I prefer to call them the "chorus of old jurors," a small
nod to Aristophanes and his play titled simply *The Wasps*.

In fifth grade, our science teacher, a dusty old nun,
taught us that wasps stun their prey and masticate them
so as to restrain them, their young then devouring them.

I found this grossly inefficient. Why chew anything
you have no intention of eating? Outside the window,
a lone wasp goes about its business of architecture.

I would like to research exactly how a wasp builds its nest,
but I know this will only make it more difficult for me
to ever again regard this act of the wasp as mysterious.

There you have it: despite my love of science, I still,
at times, prefer mystery over certainty. In Swannanoa,
one hot summer years ago, the only certainty I had was pain

and the resulting swelling in my neck from a wasp, its
wretched stinger having punctured a small tributary from my
left carotid artery. Truly, the pain was far worse

than the golf-ball-sized swelling as the blood filled
the soft tissues in my neck. It was just another of God's
small reminders to pay attention, just a small warning.

Judge and jury, the Emperor and his Senate, the King and his
Privy Council: always a system for proclaiming judgments.
The wasp, too, knows a thing or two about issuing judgments.

Portrait in Burnt Orange and Bitter Almonds

Perhaps to escape violence or war, to escape
living in one tiny room . . . on a ship from Spain,

on a ship from Hong Kong, on a ship from India,
my great-grandparents left the countries of their birth

to travel for opportunity, for safety, for love.
Yes, for love, because members of my family have

a penchant for marrying people their parents deem
"inappropriate": a Chinese cook marrying an Indian

maidservant; an indentured Spaniard marrying
a Puerto Rican Taino woman; and so on. Even the two

of us, two men marrying each other. Sitting on a terrace
overlooking Lake Como, we were nothing more

than minor nobility, something only my English
great-grandparents understood. On my father's side,

regardless of origin, poverty. You sipped grappa,
and I chose to sip amaretto, the warm orange liquid

made from the almond but better for the digestive tract
than the other potion brewed from almonds. I called it

my poison, despite the fact I knew full well it was not
cyanide. All of my paternal ancestors would have worked

on this estate as servants, as gardeners, as handymen.
Love makes people mad, my love. It asks of a man

or woman to leave one's family, one's country,
all for the sake of the beloved. For centuries, *immigrant*

has been a dirty word, but I am an immigrant, the result of
four generations of immigrants. I watch the horizon, the sun

setting, in much the way my ancestors did, with a foolish sense
of hope and an irreconcilable sadness, with the knowledge

a sunset is a sunset in any land, regardless of where you call home.

Las Palmas Reales

Playa del Carmen, Mexico

I.

The palm trees clustered together on this beach,
transplanted here almost fifty years ago,
require not even a single word of praise—
unfortunately, I am not like these palms.
The bluish-green Caribbean creates no sense
of urgency for them, no sense of being
common or disadvantaged. One wants to find
a shark's fin slicing clean the ocean's surface
but finds, instead, the light of late afternoon
arriving. It has always been this way.
The tourists are captivated by a boy
who chops the head of a coconut clean off
and drinks the water hidden within its dark
and solid husk. Amazing, they say. But this,
this is as common as salt, as common as rain.

II.

As common as salt, as common as rain, the girls
along the shore sell not beads but the idea that one
can own a part of this place, an idea as old
as Isabella, who needed to fill her coffers
with more than gold, who asked her maidens to sew
the bright and colorful feathers of birds brought back,
and offered as gifts to Spain, along the border
of her new dress. These things were easier then.
Los blancos now require more than beads.
They need the smile, the bow, the deference.
I wish I didn't understand these things.
I never wanted to, but I have bowed
to men, have smiled and listened to compliments
about how well I speak their English. I have bowed.
The royal palms refuse to bow to men.

III.

The royal palms bow only for the wind.
The coral keeps its many secrets hidden
from all except the fish that recognize
the rippling of the coral as their own.
Within an hour, the sun will set, and now
the tourists gather up their things and saunter
back to their well-appointed rooms and suites.
Tonight, at dinner, they will lament the sauce
they find too spicy, too foreign, too odd.
I need a drink. I order something cold.
Along the bar, two snails inching toward
a wilting potted plant. Dos caracoles,
I say, betraying I am gente, too.
Even before the Spanish words, the barkeep knew.
Mestizo: even proper English could not hide me.

PRECATIO SIMPLEX

in memoriam Mavis Clarke

Father, Holy Father, Prime Mover, God Almighty—
I have forgotten what to call you. Standing here
before the Pacific, I am tempted to call you

Poseidon, Green Neptune, someone I understand
more clearly than I have ever understood You.
The sea's slow tide, its almost-hidden riptide dragging

handfuls of foam under the surface, has no answers
for me. Sitting here on the crest of the sand dunes,
there is no one by my side. I have come here

alone because I remember what the nuns
taught me, that You do not appreciate a show
of these things. Not success with words, not

the lottery prize now worth millions, not the
usual things I am sure others request: I come now
to ask for something unthinkable for one like me.

Almost 3,000 miles away, near the brighter coast
of this godless country, my aunt's pain is
outpacing the cancer tearing her abdomen apart.

No amount of morphine can break it. I do not
come to ask You for miracles. I know better
than to ask for miracles. I know the world

is filled with miracles. No, no, not miracles.
Take her right now, Father. Here stands the cancer doctor
asking you to take his aunt because he cannot stomach

the idea of her in so much pain. Send me a small sign:
wheeling gulls, a sudden gust of wind, anything. Anything.
Just this once, Holy Father, don't let me down.

On Nomenclature

But it was only slightly more realistic than searching
for the Holy Grail, by which I mean it was utterly ridiculous.
On a small ship, sailing to Lima, we were told repeatedly

to keep an eye out for the Blue-footed Booby. Even the name
seemed outrageous—but nature assigned no such moniker,
humans did. The Blue-footed Booby, we were told, is

often sighted plunging head first into the sea here and, yes,
it really does have light blue feet, brighter in youth
and a duller blue as the birds age. Nature invented ageism

and, apparently, humans invented preposterous names.
Case in point: the woman who, minutes after I delivered
her baby girl, announced she would be named Marksalot.

She named her daughter after the fluorescent highlighter
on her bed stand. Out over a gunmetal sea, there was not
a bird in sight: no pelicans, no gulls, and not a single

Blue-footed Booby. Despite hours of staring through tiny
binoculars, we never saw one. We saw only waves.
It has been years since that day sailing into Lima,

and I couldn't explain to you exactly why this memory
decided to present itself to me now, except that here,
out over the Pacific, not a single bird can be seen. Instead,

we have the Blue Angels thundering out over the Golden Gate
practicing for their Fleet Week show tomorrow. The jets
don't really seem that blue, so I have to assume

they are old. And though they stream through the skies,
nothing about them seems angelic. And I wonder
if there is something angelic about the Blue-footed Booby.

Like angels, they are rare and rarely seen. One must be
desperate, I believe, to see one, the way poor Joseph was
when an angel of the Lord appeared to him to ensure

he understood his wife was carrying the Son of God.
Joseph named the child Jesus, though I am told it was really
Yeshua. One of them means *rare*, means *worth more than gold*.

Cancer

in memoriam Paul Otremba

One must be trained to locate it. One finds it
by finding the Lion first and then the Brothers.
The faintest of the thirteen signs in the night sky,

we have learned to see it by discerning what flanks it.
You were right that evening in Vermont to say
it doesn't even look like a crab. I joked it looked

more like an upside-down Y, more like the Greek
λ, a symbol which, for me, had more to do with
radioactivity calculations used in radiation therapy.

I was showing off, you see, making sure I would be seen
as a doctor as well as a writer. But by then we were
already close enough for you to forgive my arrogance.

But your question came quickly: *How do you do it*
every day? All those people with cancer... We stared
at the stars, and I recounted a sordid story

about an old poet we admired. The stars,
the resulting story, and your laughter: the things
memory made indelible. You knew it was the veins

spreading out in a solid tumor seen when cut and examined
that reminded Hippocrates of the crab, something
far less poetic than the stars seen in the night sky,

but that is how you chose to think about it. And because
oncologists always think of cancer, I purposely chose
to think of reflux when, over lunch two years ago, you

kept coughing, kept choking. Later, you told me
that as you lay in the scanner you loved the idea of light
passing through you, photons used to look inside your chest.

Even then, you chose the poetic. Your greatest fear
was that the biopsy might discover an ulcer leading to
restrictions on fine food and wine. Instead, they found the crab.

You were born under the sign of the scorpion, but I
always saw you as a Lion. A brother, I assumed you were safely
distanced from the crab. Let the light pass through you now.

Not the photons we manipulate for Medicine,
but the starlight that has traveled with us for millennia.
We need not look for the Lion or the Brothers anymore.

Portrait in Ochre and Seven Whispers

i.

To make and remake one's self is
the artist's job, I believed. And so, in poems,
I gave myself wings. But even then, I made sure
the wings could not support flight, could not
lift me to safety. Even my imagination failed me.

ii.

The first time I tried to kill myself, I swallowed
a bottle of Tylenol, pill after pill, like the sacrament
of communion, placed on my tongue.

iii.

You were supposed to save us. You were
supposed to help save our souls. Isn't that part
of the vow you made to God when choosing
the life you did? You must have forgotten that.
You didn't kill my soul. But you didn't save it either.

iv.

I'm never late anymore, never late to anything.
Because I still wonder if I hadn't dawdled after practice,
if I had showered with the other boys instead of
waiting, if... There are always so many *ifs*.
Would you have stopped if I had screamed, if I had
fought harder? I still find it so easy to list off the *ifs*.

v.

My second lie came when I woke, in the hospital,
and told my parents I swallowed the pills
because I was being bullied at school.
An easy lie. Much easier than the truth. The third lie?
The promise I would never try to kill myself again.

vi.

The woman killing my parents, the sudden
and uncontrolled rising from the ground as people
gawked and screamed, the vomiting up of gold coins:
dreams I have had repeatedly over all these years.

vii.

I found your obituary, the memorial, the pictures
of you as a kindly old priest. You are dead now.
I wanted to write my own statement for you,
to shame you, to tell the world how you pinned
the thirteen-year-old me to the wall in a gym's shower,
put your hands around my neck, and sodomized me.
But shame is never an equal transaction, is it? Shame,
the one thing I cannot live with, cannot live without.

Portrait in Graphite and Ornamental Hagiography

You may not believe it, but I have tried,
set my sights on the morning star
in belief it would guide me. I have tried.

I have tried, as the Jesuits taught, to be
singular, to be whole, to be one. The labor
of this was exhausting. Time reveals things

one need not appreciate when young, and I fear
being singular, being one, is something
damned near impossible for someone

like me. Saint Jerome, cloistered in a tiny room,
found his singular calling in updating
the Latin Bible with his knowledge of Greek texts.

In Assisi, Saint Francis updated nature, called birds
out of the trees. I am, unfortunately, no saint.
Fractured, divided to the quick, I am incapable

of being singular. And the old nun who taught Art
at my high school, who called me a stupid mongrel,
understood this very fact long before I did.

Profession, family, belief: I can see now
my background challenges me, prevents me
from remaining true to only one thing. The fog,

settled over Ocean Beach, settles the matter
by embracing everything indiscriminately,
and I want to understand why I notice

such things. For most of my life, I have desired
a category, a designation, but maybe
that desire was misplaced? Maybe it was just

another failure, a failure of imagination?
Outside, two hummingbirds cross-stitch the air.
They have lived here for so long, lived

off the "nectar" I boil up for them each week,
that they show me no semblance of fear or distrust—
they hover and feed near me with violent precision.

Prometeo

∞

The cane field owns you. You own the cane field.
You never stole fire, you created it.

∞

A convex or flat bevel, from spine to edge,
a secondary bevel to have a slight distal taper—
resistant to chipping and breaking,

the blade must be tempered not heat-treated
the way common knives are. It stands up to
repeated impacts. It does not easily break if abused.

∞

Nothing is ever as simple as it appears.
You know this. Whether held by the farmer
or the guerrilla, your clean, sharp surface
is but an extension of the arm.
How many times have men tried to make
of you a symbol only to fail?

∞

My father cleared an acre quicker than
a machine with nothing more than a machete.

∞

When you speak to us, you
speak Español—but you are
fluent in Armenian, Malaysian,
Thai, Portuguese, Tagalog,
and numerous languages
from the African continent.

∞

Weapon of choice for uprisings, we so desired you
we adopted your name, became Macheteros.

∞

I imagine the carbon springs to life under the hammer,
the edge sharpened to starshine. Striking rock with it
kindles fires, its sparks numerous and bright.
There was always fire within the machete.

∞

Strange inheritance, one I denied for so long.
I listen to you daily even though you say little.
Next to you, I can still smell the fire of sugar.

Portrait in Nightshade and Delayed Translation

In Saint Petersburg, on an autumn morning,
having been allowed an early entry
to the Hermitage, my family and I wandered
the empty hallways and corridors, virtually every space

adorned with famous paintings and artwork.
There must be a term for overloading on art.
One of Caravaggio's boys smirked at us,
his lips a red that betrayed a sloppy kiss

recently delivered, while across the room
the Virgin looked on with nothing but sorrow.
Even in museums, the drama is staged.
Bored, I left my family and, steered myself,

foolish moth, toward the light coming
from a rotunda. Before me, the empty stairs.
Ready to descend, ready to step outside
into the damp and chilly air, I felt

the centuries-old reflex kick in, that sense
of being watched. When I turned, I found
no one; instead, I was staring at *The Return
of the Prodigal Son*. I had studied it, written about it

as a student. But no amount of study could have
prepared me for the size of it, the darkness of it.
There, the son knelt before his father, his dirty foot
left for inspection. Something broke. As clichéd

as it sounds, something inside me broke, and
as if captured on film, I found myself slowly sinking
to my knees. The tears began without warning until soon
I was sobbing. What reflex betrays one like this?

What nerve agent did Rembrandt hide
within the dark shades of paint that he used?
What inside me had malfunctioned, had left me
kneeling and sobbing in a museum?

Prosto plakat. Prosto plakat. Osvobodi sebya,
said the guard as his hands steadied my shoulders.
He stood there repeating the phrase until
I stopped crying, until I was able to rise.

I'm not crazy, nor am I a very emotional man.
For most of my life, I have been called, correctly, cold.
As a student, I catalogued the techniques, carefully
analyzed this painting for a class on the "Dutch Masters."

Years later, having mustered the courage to tell
this ridiculous story, a friend who spoke Russian
translated the guard's words for me: *Just cry. Just cry.*
Free yourself. But free myself from what, exactly?

You see, I want this whole thing to be something
meaningful, my falling to my knees in front of a painting
by Rembrandt, a painting inspired by a parable
of forgiveness offered by a father to his lost son.

But nothing meaningful has presented itself. Even now,
after so much time has passed, I have no clue
what any of this means. I still haven't figured out
whether or not I am the lost son or the found.

Between the Dragon and the Phoenix

Fire in the heart, fire in the sky, the sun just
a smallish smudge resting on the horizon
out beyond the reef that breaks the waves,

fiery sun that waits for no one. I was little more
than a child when my father explained
that the mongrel is stronger than the thoroughbred,

that I was splendidly blended, genetically engineered
for survival. I somehow forgot this, misplaced this,
time eroding my memory as it erodes everything.

But go ask someone else to write a poem about Time.
Out over the bay, the sun is rising, and I am running
out of time. Each and every year, on my birthday,

I wake to watch the sunrise. I am superstitious.
And today, as in years past, it is not my father
but my father's father who comes to shout at me:

Whether you like it or not, you are a child of fire. You
descend from the Dragon, descend from the Phoenix.
Your blood is older than England, older than Castille.

Year after year, he says the same thing, this old man
dead long before I was born. So, I wake each year
on the day of my birth to watch the fire enter the sky

while being chastised by my dead grandfather.
Despite being a creature of fire, I stay near the water.
Why even try to avoid what can extinguish me?

There are times I can feel the fire flickering inside my frame.
The gulls are quarreling, the palm trees shimmering—
the world keeps spinning on its axis. Some say I have

nine lives. Others think me a machine. Neither is true.
The truth is rarely so conventional. Fire in my heart, fire
in my veins, I write this down for you and watch

as it goes up in flames. There are no paragraphs
wide enough to contain this fire, no stanzas
durable enough to house it. Blood of the Dragon,

blood of the Phoenix, I turn my head slowly
toward the East. I bow and call for another year.
I stand there and demand one more year.

Acknowledgments

Grateful acknowledgment is made to the editors of the following publications, where these poems—sometimes in slightly different forms—first appeared:

Academy of American Poets' *Poem-a-Day*, *American Poetry Review*, *Bennington Review*, *Blackbird*, *The Collagist*, *Four Way Review*, *Literary Matters*, *Maggy*, *New England Review*, *The New Republic*, *Orion*, *Plume*, *Scoundrel Time*, *storySouth*, *Tin House*, and *Waxwing*.

"*Precatio simplex*" was reprinted in *The Best American Poetry 2017*, ed. Natasha Trethewey, series ed. David Lehman. (Scribner, 2017)

As always, I would like to thank my beloved, Jacob Bertrand. I would also like to thank my family and friends for the support, both large and small, they have given me. I also want to thank my editor Martha Rhodes and all of the people that constitute Four Way Books for their continued support of my work.

C. Dale Young practices medicine full-time. He is the author of *The Affliction* (Four Way Books, 2018), a novel in stories, and the poetry collections *The Day Underneath the Day* (Northwestern, 2001); *The Second Person* (Four Way Books, 2007), a finalist for the Lambda Literary Award in Poetry; *Torn* (Four Way Books, 2011), named one of the best poetry collections of 2011 by National Public Radio; and *The Halo* (Four Way Books, 2016). He is a previous recipient of the Grolier Prize, the Stanley W. Lindberg Award for Literary Editing, and the 2017/2018 Hanes Award in Poetry given by the Fellowship of Southern Writers to honor a poet at mid-career. Young is a fellow of the National Endowment for the Arts, the John Simon Guggenheim Memorial Foundation, and the Rockefeller Foundation, and his poems and short fiction have appeared widely. He lives in San Francisco.

Publication of this book was made possible by grants and donations. We are also grateful to those individuals who participated in our 2020 Build a Book Program. They are:

Anonymous (14), Robert Abrams, Nancy Allen, Maggie Anderson, Sally Ball, Matt Bell, Laurel Blossom, Adam Bohannon, Lee Briccetti, Therese Broderick, Jane Martha Brox, Christopher Bursk, Liam Callanan, Anthony Cappo, Carla & Steven Carlson, Paul & Brandy Carlson, Renee Carlson, Cyrus Cassells, Robin Rosen Chang, Jaye Chen, Edward W. Clark, Andrea Cohen, Ellen Cosgrove, Peter Coyote, Janet S. Crossen, Kim & David Daniels, Brian Komei Dempster, Matthew DeNichilo, Carl Dennis, Patrick Donnelly, Charles Douthat, Morgan Driscoll, Lynn Emanuel, Monica Ferrell, Elliot Figman, Laura Fjeld, Michael Foran, Jennifer Franklin, Sarah Freligh, Helen Fremont & Donna Thagard, Reginald Gibbons, Jean & Jay Glassman, Ginny Gordon, Lauri Grossman, Naomi Guttman & Jonathan Mead, Mark Halliday, Beth Harrison, Jeffrey Harrison, Page Hill Starzinger, Deming Holleran, Joan Houlihan, Thomas & Autumn Howard, Elizabeth Jackson, Christopher Johanson, Voki Kalfayan, Maeve Kinkead, David Lee, Jen Levitt, Howard Levy, Owen Lewis, Jennifer Litt, Sara London & Dean Albarelli, David Long, James Longenbach, Excelsior Love, Ralph & Mary Ann Lowen, Jacquelyn Malone, Donna Masini, Catherine McArthur, Nathan McClain, Richard McCormick, Victoria McCoy, Ellen McCulloch-Lovell, Judith McGrath, Debbie & Steve Modzelewski, Rajiv Mohabir, James T. F. Moore, Beth Morris, John Murillo & Nicole Sealey, Michael & Nancy Murphy, Maria Nazos, Kimberly Nunes, Bill O'Brien, Susan Okie & Walter Weiss, Rebecca Okrent, Sam Perkins, Megan Pinto, Kyle Potvin, Glen Pourciau, Kevin Prufer, Barbara Ras, Victoria Redel, Martha Rhodes, Paula Rhodes, Paula Ristuccia, George & Nancy Rosenfeld, M. L. Samios, Peter & Jill Schireson, Rob Schlegel, Roni & Richard Schotter, Jane Scovell, Andrew Seligsohn & Martina Anderson, James & Nancy Shalek, Soraya Shalforoosh, Peggy Shinner, Dara-Lyn Shrager, Joan Silber, Emily Sinclair, James Snyder & Krista Fragos, Alice St. Claire-Long, Megan Staffel, Bonnie Stetson, Yerra Sugarman, Dorothy Tapper Goldman, Marjorie & Lew Tesser, Earl Teteak, Parker & Phyllis Towle, Pauline Uchmanowicz, Rosalynde Vas Dias, Connie Voisine, Valerie Wallace, Doris Warriner, Ellen Doré Watson, Martha Webster & Robert Fuentes, Calvin Wei, Bill Wenthe, Allison Benis White, Michelle Whittaker, and Ira Zapin.